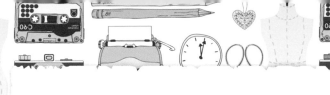

Lists—some people live by them, others scorn them. Chances are if you have picked up this journal, you are in the first group. But do your lists begin and end with the day's tasks, all to be ticked off before your head hits the pillow in the evening? It's natural to be focused on the everyday realities of life, but sometimes it can be valuable to stop, take time out, and remember the people and places you've loved, the activities in which you can escape, and the adventures you would like to go on—these personal reflections and aspirations can form new lists to guide you to a more creative, more mindful, and more fulfilling future.

This list journal is divided into five sections—*Escape, Living, Mindfulness, Creativity,* and *Well-being*—each of which provides you with the opportunity to explore the past, present, and future. It can be opened at any page of any section and used as a done-that as well as a would-like-to-do guide to help you achieve your goals and live your dreams.

There are also pages for you to create your own lists, ask questions, and note down ideas while extra room has been left for you to describe the music, literature, events, and people who have made up the significant chapters in your life.

BE CREATIVE. Personalize your lists. Add photos of family, friends, and special places, stick in theater and exhibition tickets, and draw pictures of your dream house, favorite flower, or much-loved pet.

BE INTERESTED. Use the sidebars to scribble the names of colleges or community centers where you can try a new craft, websites that will help you plan your next museum trip, or names of people who could put you in touch with a long-lost friend.

BE MINDFUL. As you reflect and record your feelings, ambitions and hopes, be proud of how far you have come—every achievement, no matter how big or small, is significant—and excited about how far you could go.

Relax and enjoy the process. It is your life, they are your lists—and you can add, change, and tick them off in your own space and in your own time.

Breathe Magazine
breathemagazine.co.uk

Escape

My favorite places to escape and make time for myself

....

....

....

....

....

....

....

....

....

....

....

....

....

....

....

Remember . . . give yourself some space. Solitude is a powerful aid to silence and gives your brain a rest from constant distractions, a chance to reflect and gain a greater appreciation of who you are and what makes your life special.

Things I could do if I were brave enough

Unscripted moment

Describe a spontaneous action that led to something unexpected

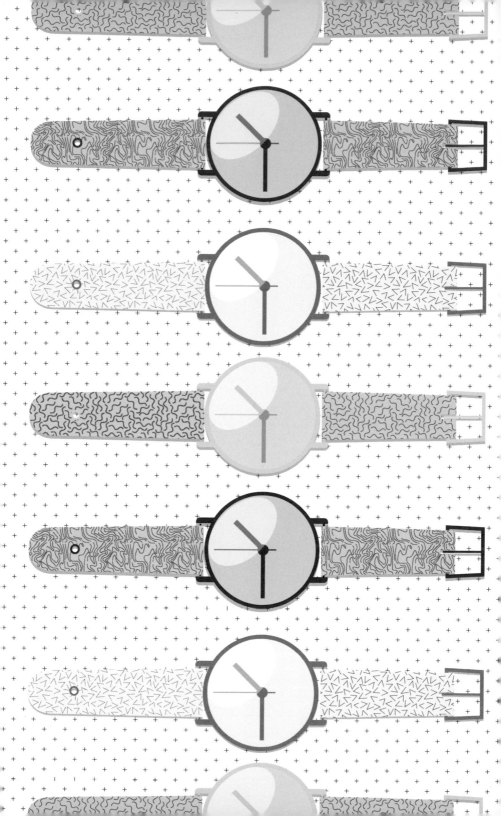

Things I would do if I had a spare afternoon

Things I would do if I had a spare weekend

My best day

Describe the moments, people, and places that made up 24 perfect hours

"*To sit in the shade on a fine day, and look upon verdure is the most perfect refreshment*"

Jane Austen, author

What I enjoy most about the outdoors

My favorite spot

Describe a special place and explain why it means so much

The most beautiful places I have seen

Activities in which I escape

_____

_____

_____

_____

_____

_____

_____

_____

_____

_____

_____

_____

_____

Remember... practice mindfulness in everyday activities. If you're a walker or runner, focus on the feel of the sidewalk beneath your feet, the coolness of the air entering your lungs, the scent of a rose bush you pass by. Don't just check the exercise off your to-do list—imagine it's the first time you have ever been out walking or running.

My best trip...

My ultimate adventure from start to finish

Cities I would like to explore

Living

"*Home is the nicest word there is*"

Laura Ingalls Wilder,
author

Places I would like to live

My dream home

Top to bottom and inside out, describe the essentials for the perfect abode

Weekend projects I could complete in the next year

What do I need to declutter?

"Have nothing in your house that you do not know to be useful, or believe to be beautiful"

William Morris,
textile designer

Healthy eating habits I would like to adopt

Did you know? Researchers at Duke University
in North Carolina estimate that habits account
for 45 percent of everyday behaviors.

Recipes I would like to master

Foods I should eat more often

Things I would like to grow

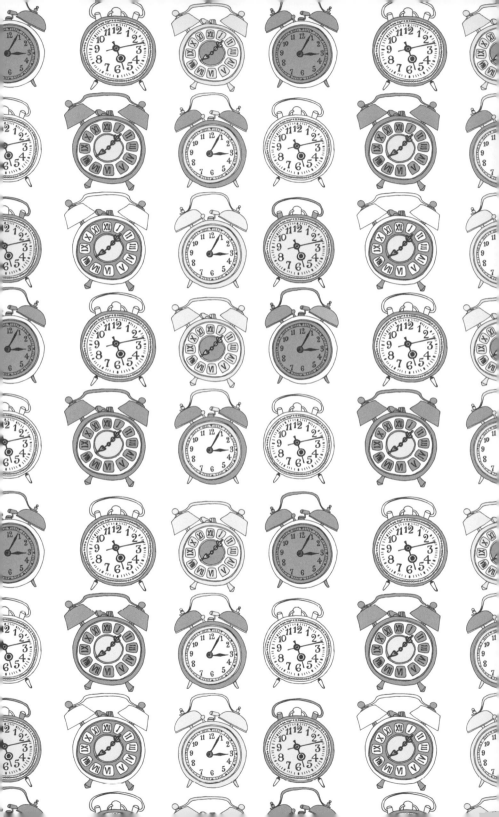

My daily routines and ways I could
make them more fulfilling

Mindfulness

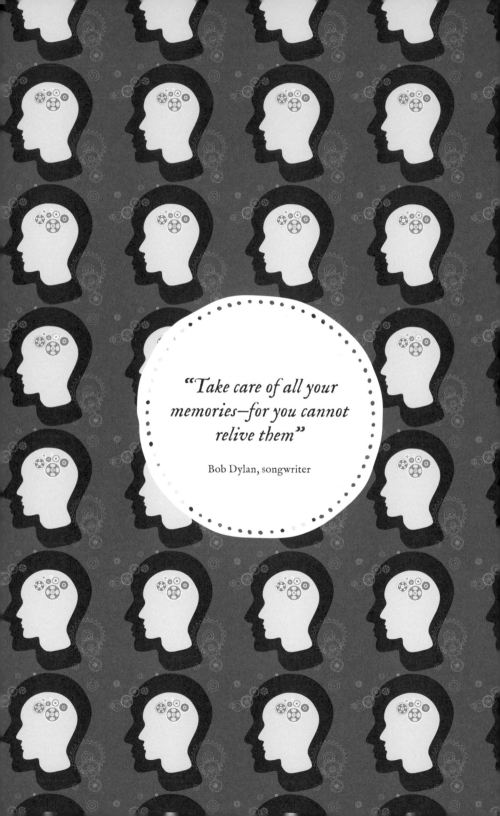

"*Take care of all your memories—for you cannot relive them*"

Bob Dylan, songwriter

My proudest moments

The achievements—big and small—
that have made me feel happy

Times I've exceeded
my own expectations

Remember... if you have a voice in your head saying you are
not all you could be, replace it with one that says "I AM ENOUGH."
Say it every morning and evening until your mind accepts it.

Things I would like to learn or revisit

Quotations and sayings I love

THE BEST WAY

TO PREDICT THE

future

IS

TO CREATE IT

Once upon a time...

Write down passages from books that have become firm favorites

My favorite books and authors

Books to read

Things that bring me serenity and calmness

My ideal job would be . . .

If I didn't have to work, I would like to . . .

My favorite poets and poems

My number one poem

From first line to last, write down a poem that feeds the soul

My fears and ways I can overcome them

....

....

....

....

....

....

....

....

....

....

....

....

....

....

Remember . . . negative thoughts, feelings, and self-destructive behaviors often get in the way of accomplishing what we really desire. It's called self-sabotage. Switch your internal dialogue from negative to positive, and break through your comfort zone to make change happen.

Things that cause me stress

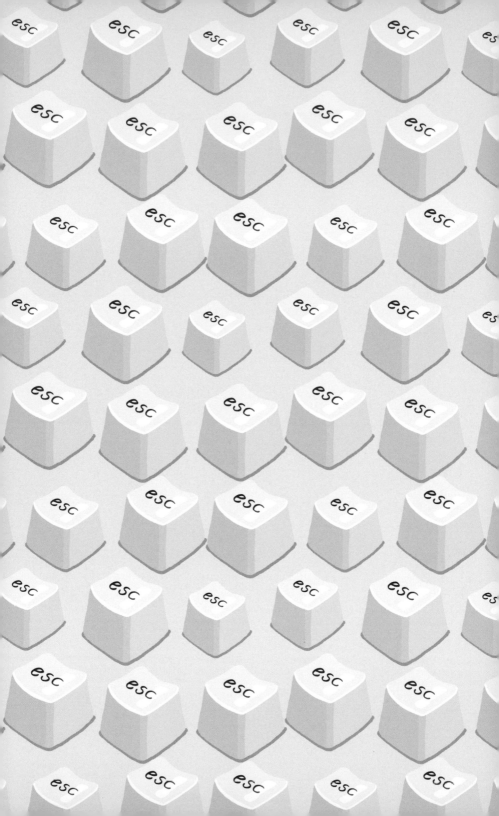

Things I would miss during a digital detox

Movies that influenced me

Scene stealers

If my life were made into a movie, these would be the key moments

My dreams

"All that we see or seem is but a dream within a dream"

Edgar Allan Poe,
writer

Creativity

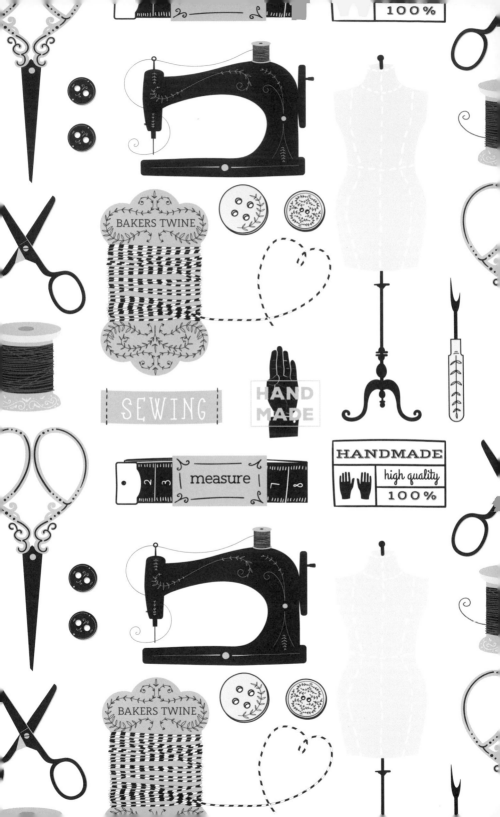

Crafts I would like to try

Be proud . . . whether you're working on a big project that will take months to complete, or a quick fix that leaves you with a beautifully finished object, take time to look at your work, enjoy it, and acknowledge what you have accomplished.

New materials to explore and new techniques to learn

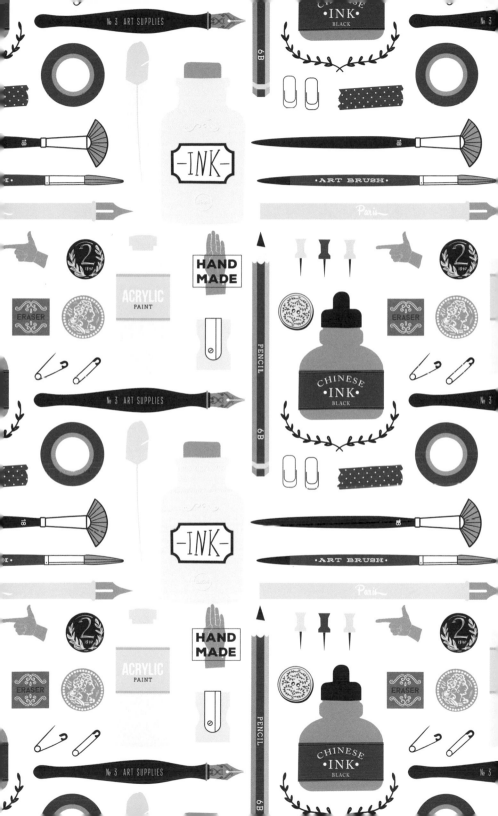

People or artists who have inspired me

Museums I would like to visit

Places or people I would like to photograph

Remember... mindfulness is about being fully awake and alive. It's about experiencing life moments without wishing things could be different. If this attitude leads to heightened visual awareness, improved concentration, and more rewarding photography then so be it. These outcomes should be by-products rather than end goals. Keep a receptive mind, stop looking, and start seeing.

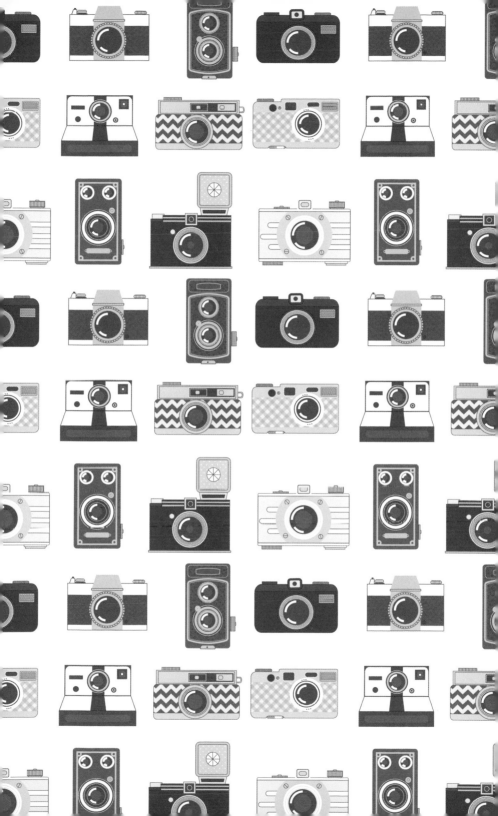

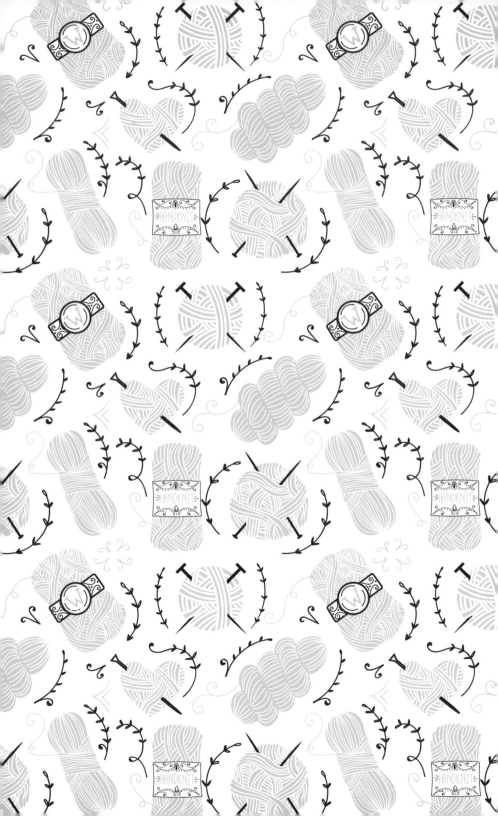

Gifts I would like to make for friends

Words I would like to use more often

"*The most important thing is to read as much as you can . . . it will give you an understanding of what makes good writing and it will enlarge your vocabulary*"

JK Rowling, author

Ideas and inspirations for a novel or short story

Remember . . . start at the beginning. What is the germ of your idea? Is it an anecdote, an encounter, a scene, a sentence, or something else? Begin here, then explore.

How I think the world will look in the future

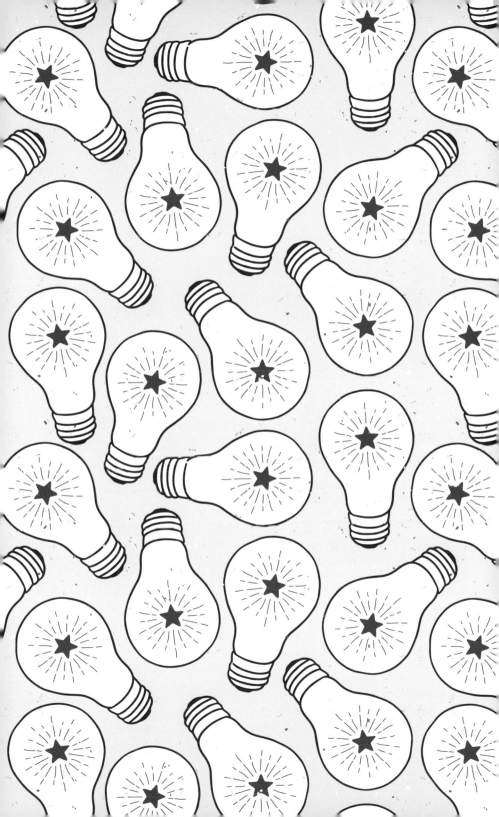

Well-being

People I would like to reconnect with

People I admire

My favorite someone

Describe the one person who makes life special

Things I treasure most in the world

Things I wish someone had told me earlier

The best advice I have ever been given

Music that relaxes me

"*Music, once admitted to the soul, becomes a sort of spirit, and never dies*"

Edward Bulwer-Lytton,
writer and politician

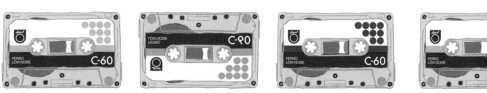

Moments I should savor—and why

_____

_____

_____

_____

_____

_____

_____

_____

_____

_____

_____

_____

_____

_____

_____

_____

Remember . . . think about what good things lie ahead for you, whether it's some time in the future—like going on vacation—or something imminent like an evening with your book and a hot bath. Imagine what the experience will be like, what you'll do, and how you'll feel.

Ways to nurture my well-being

Remember . . . laughing uses muscles and that exertion releases endorphins, reducing physical and psychological stress. You breathe deeper, too, which means your lungs get a good workout as well.

Treats that thrill me

Good wishes I'd like to send myself

Things to look forward to in the future

Things I would like to let go

Things I could do to express gratitude

Little things that bring me joy

"*You need to let the little things that would ordinarily bore you, suddenly thrill you*"

Andy Warhol, artist

The process of recalling the past, being mindful about the present, and contemplating the future takes time, self-awareness, and honesty. You've done it and your lists will always be here for further reflection. But, there's no need to stop! Writing lists is a useful way to understand what's going on in life—any time a new idea comes to mind, note it here . . .

STERLING
New York

An Imprint of Sterling Publishing, Co., Inc.
1166 Avenue of the Americas
New York, NY 10016

ISBN 978-1-4549-3177-5

Distributed in Canada by Sterling Publishing Co., Inc.
c/o Canadian Manda Group, 664 Annette Street
Toronto, Ontario M6S 2C8, Canada

For information about custom editions, special sales, and premium and
corporate purchases, please contact Sterling Special Sales at 800-805-5489
or specialsales@sterlingpublishing.com.

Manufactured in Canada

2 4 6 8 10 9 7 5 3 1

sterlingpublishing.com

All images courtesy of shutterstock.com